2021

HOMEMAKER'S FRIEND

*daily*planner

SUE HOOLEY

The 2021 Homemaker's Friend Daily Planner

is dedicated to my sisters,

RACHEL DOUTRICH, KEREN STEINER, AND JEWEL BIRKY.

We did it! And we are still friends.

You girls are the best.

2021 DAILY PLANNER

Christian Light Publications, Inc.
Harrisonburg, Virginia 22802

© 2020 Christian Light Publications, Inc.
All rights reserved.
Printed in China.

ISBN: 978-0-87813-320-8

To order planners by mail, please use order form in back.
Your comments and suggestions are welcomed!

Cover Design: Lanette Steiner
Text Design: Rhoda Miller & Lanette Steiner

A SPECIAL NOTE OF THANKS
TO KATHERINE DERSTINE
for choosing the Scripture verses.
THE VERSES CONTAIN THE THEME OF GROWING AND FLOWING.

THIS **DAILY PLANNER** BELONGS TO:

_____

_____

_____

_____

_____

IMPORTANT PHONE NUMBERS:

NAME   PHONE

_____   _____

_____   _____

_____   _____

_____   _____

_____   _____

_____   _____

_____   _____

_____   _____

BUT *grow in grace,*
AND IN THE KNOWLEDGE OF OUR LORD. II PETER 3:18

TWO THOUSAND TWENTY

JANUARY 2020
S	M	T	W	T	F	S
			1	2	3	4
5	6	7	8	9	10	11
12	13	14	15	16	17	18
19	20	21	22	23	24	25
26	27	28	29	30	31	

FEBRUARY 2020
S	M	T	W	T	F	S
						1
2	3	4	5	6	7	8
9	10	11	12	13	14	15
16	17	18	19	20	21	22
23	24	25	26	27	28	29

MARCH 2020
S	M	T	W	T	F	S
1	2	3	4	5	6	7
8	9	10	11	12	13	14
15	16	17	18	19	20	21
22	23	24	25	26	27	28
29	30	31				

APRIL 2020
S	M	T	W	T	F	S
			1	2	3	4
5	6	7	8	9	10	11
12	13	14	15	16	17	18
19	20	21	22	23	24	25
26	27	28	29	30		

MAY 2020
S	M	T	W	T	F	S
					1	2
3	4	5	6	7	8	9
10	11	12	13	14	15	16
17	18	19	20	21	22	23
24	25	26	27	28	29	30
31						

JUNE 2020
S	M	T	W	T	F	S
	1	2	3	4	5	6
7	8	9	10	11	12	13
14	15	16	17	18	19	20
21	22	23	24	25	26	27
28	29	30				

JULY 2020
S	M	T	W	T	F	S
			1	2	3	4
5	6	7	8	9	10	11
12	13	14	15	16	17	18
19	20	21	22	23	24	25
26	27	28	29	30	31	

AUGUST 2020
S	M	T	W	T	F	S
						1
2	3	4	5	6	7	8
9	10	11	12	13	14	15
16	17	18	19	20	21	22
23	24	25	26	27	28	29
30	31					

SEPTEMBER 2020
S	M	T	W	T	F	S
		1	2	3	4	5
6	7	8	9	10	11	12
13	14	15	16	17	18	19
20	21	22	23	24	25	26
27	28	29	30			

OCTOBER 2020
S	M	T	W	T	F	S
				1	2	3
4	5	6	7	8	9	10
11	12	13	14	15	16	17
18	19	20	21	22	23	24
25	26	27	28	29	30	31

NOVEMBER 2020
S	M	T	W	T	F	S
1	2	3	4	5	6	7
8	9	10	11	12	13	14
15	16	17	18	19	20	21
22	23	24	25	26	27	28
29	30					

DECEMBER 2020
S	M	T	W	T	F	S
		1	2	3	4	5
6	7	8	9	10	11	12
13	14	15	16	17	18	19
20	21	22	23	24	25	26
27	28	29	30	31		

TWO THOUSAND TWENTY-ONE

JANUARY 2021
S	M	T	W	T	F	S
					1	2
3	4	5	6	7	8	9
10	11	12	13	14	15	16
17	18	19	20	21	22	23
24	25	26	27	28	29	30
31						

FEBRUARY 2021
S	M	T	W	T	F	S
	1	2	3	4	5	6
7	8	9	10	11	12	13
14	15	16	17	18	19	20
21	22	23	24	25	26	27
28						

MARCH 2021
S	M	T	W	T	F	S
	1	2	3	4	5	6
7	8	9	10	11	12	13
14	15	16	17	18	19	20
21	22	23	24	25	26	27
28	29	30	31			

APRIL 2021
S	M	T	W	T	F	S
				1	2	3
4	5	6	7	8	9	10
11	12	13	14	15	16	17
18	19	20	21	22	23	24
25	26	27	28	29	30	

MAY 2021
S	M	T	W	T	F	S
						1
2	3	4	5	6	7	8
9	10	11	12	13	14	15
16	17	18	19	20	21	22
23	24	25	26	27	28	29
30	31					

JUNE 2021
S	M	T	W	T	F	S
		1	2	3	4	5
6	7	8	9	10	11	12
13	14	15	16	17	18	19
20	21	22	23	24	25	26
27	28	29	30			

JULY 2021
S	M	T	W	T	F	S
				1	2	3
4	5	6	7	8	9	10
11	12	13	14	15	16	17
18	19	20	21	22	23	24
25	26	27	28	29	30	31

AUGUST 2021
S	M	T	W	T	F	S
1	2	3	4	5	6	7
8	9	10	11	12	13	14
15	16	17	18	19	20	21
22	23	24	25	26	27	28
29	30	31				

SEPTEMBER 2021
S	M	T	W	T	F	S
			1	2	3	4
5	6	7	8	9	10	11
12	13	14	15	16	17	18
19	20	21	22	23	24	25
26	27	28	29	30		

OCTOBER 2021
S	M	T	W	T	F	S
					1	2
3	4	5	6	7	8	9
10	11	12	13	14	15	16
17	18	19	20	21	22	23
24	25	26	27	28	29	30
31						

NOVEMBER 2021
S	M	T	W	T	F	S
	1	2	3	4	5	6
7	8	9	10	11	12	13
14	15	16	17	18	19	20
21	22	23	24	25	26	27
28	29	30				

DECEMBER 2021
S	M	T	W	T	F	S
			1	2	3	4
5	6	7	8	9	10	11
12	13	14	15	16	17	18
19	20	21	22	23	24	25
26	27	28	29	30	31	

TWO THOUSAND **TWENTY-TWO**

JANUARY 2022
S	M	T	W	T	F	S
						1
2	3	4	5	6	7	8
9	10	11	12	13	14	15
16	17	18	19	20	21	22
23	24	25	26	27	28	29
30	31					

FEBRUARY 2022
S	M	T	W	T	F	S
		1	2	3	4	5
6	7	8	9	10	11	12
13	14	15	16	17	18	19
20	21	22	23	24	25	26
27	28					

MARCH 2022
S	M	T	W	T	F	S
		1	2	3	4	5
6	7	8	9	10	11	12
13	14	15	16	17	18	19
20	21	22	23	24	25	26
27	28	29	30	31		

APRIL 2022
S	M	T	W	T	F	S
					1	2
3	4	5	6	7	8	9
10	11	12	13	14	15	16
17	18	19	20	21	22	23
24	25	26	27	28	29	30

MAY 2022
S	M	T	W	T	F	S
1	2	3	4	5	6	7
8	9	10	11	12	13	14
15	16	17	18	19	20	21
22	23	24	25	26	27	28
29	30	31				

JUNE 2022
S	M	T	W	T	F	S
			1	2	3	4
5	6	7	8	9	10	11
12	13	14	15	16	17	18
19	20	21	22	23	24	25
26	27	28	29	30		

JULY 2022
S	M	T	W	T	F	S
					1	2
3	4	5	6	7	8	9
10	11	12	13	14	15	16
17	18	19	20	21	22	23
24	25	26	27	28	29	30
31						

AUGUST 2022
S	M	T	W	T	F	S
	1	2	3	4	5	6
7	8	9	10	11	12	13
14	15	16	17	18	19	20
21	22	23	24	25	26	27
28	29	30	31			

SEPTEMBER 2022
S	M	T	W	T	F	S
				1	2	3
4	5	6	7	8	9	10
11	12	13	14	15	16	17
18	19	20	21	22	23	24
25	26	27	28	29	30	

OCTOBER 2022
S	M	T	W	T	F	S
						1
2	3	4	5	6	7	8
9	10	11	12	13	14	15
16	17	18	19	20	21	22
23	24	25	26	27	28	29
30	31					

NOVEMBER 2022
S	M	T	W	T	F	S
		1	2	3	4	5
6	7	8	9	10	11	12
13	14	15	16	17	18	19
20	21	22	23	24	25	26
27	28	29	30			

DECEMBER 2022
S	M	T	W	T	F	S
				1	2	3
4	5	6	7	8	9	10
11	12	13	14	15	16	17
18	19	20	21	22	23	24
25	26	27	28	29	30	31

TWO THOUSAND **TWENTY-THREE**

JANUARY 2023
S	M	T	W	T	F	S
1	2	3	4	5	6	7
8	9	10	11	12	13	14
15	16	17	18	19	20	21
22	23	24	25	26	27	28
29	30	31				

FEBRUARY 2023
S	M	T	W	T	F	S
			1	2	3	4
5	6	7	8	9	10	11
12	13	14	15	16	17	18
19	20	21	22	23	24	25
26	27	28				

MARCH 2023
S	M	T	W	T	F	S
			1	2	3	4
5	6	7	8	9	10	11
12	13	14	15	16	17	18
19	20	21	22	23	24	25
26	27	28	29	30	31	

APRIL 2023
S	M	T	W	T	F	S
						1
2	3	4	5	6	7	8
9	10	11	12	13	14	15
16	17	18	19	20	21	22
23	24	25	26	27	28	29
30						

MAY 2023
S	M	T	W	T	F	S
	1	2	3	4	5	6
7	8	9	10	11	12	13
14	15	16	17	18	19	20
21	22	23	24	25	26	27
28	29	30	31			

JUNE 2023
S	M	T	W	T	F	S
				1	2	3
4	5	6	7	8	9	10
11	12	13	14	15	16	17
18	19	20	21	22	23	24
25	26	27	28	29	30	

JULY 2023
S	M	T	W	T	F	S
						1
2	3	4	5	6	7	8
9	10	11	12	13	14	15
16	17	18	19	20	21	22
23	24	25	26	27	28	29
30	31					

AUGUST 2023
S	M	T	W	T	F	S
		1	2	3	4	5
6	7	8	9	10	11	12
13	14	15	16	17	18	19
20	21	22	23	24	25	26
27	28	29	30	31		

SEPTEMBER 2023
S	M	T	W	T	F	S
					1	2
3	4	5	6	7	8	9
10	11	12	13	14	15	16
17	18	19	20	21	22	23
24	25	26	27	28	29	30

OCTOBER 2023
S	M	T	W	T	F	S
1	2	3	4	5	6	7
8	9	10	11	12	13	14
15	16	17	18	19	20	21
22	23	24	25	26	27	28
29	30	31				

NOVEMBER 2023
S	M	T	W	T	F	S
			1	2	3	4
5	6	7	8	9	10	11
12	13	14	15	16	17	18
19	20	21	22	23	24	25
26	27	28	29	30		

DECEMBER 2023
S	M	T	W	T	F	S
					1	2
3	4	5	6	7	8	9
10	11	12	13	14	15	16
17	18	19	20	21	22	23
24	25	26	27	28	29	30
31						

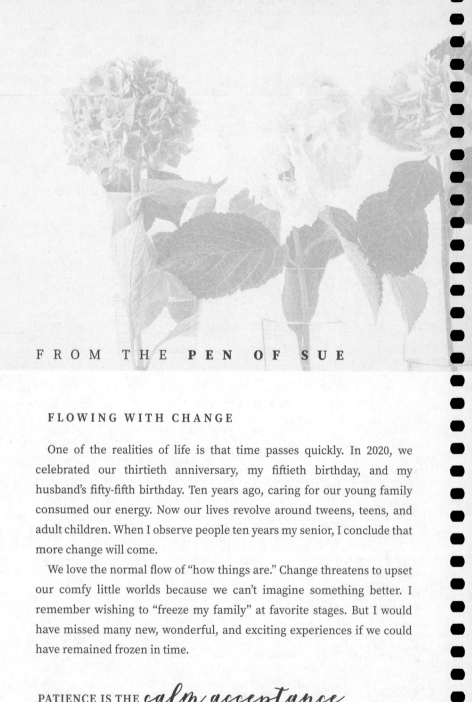

FROM THE **PEN** OF **SUE**

FLOWING WITH CHANGE

One of the realities of life is that time passes quickly. In 2020, we celebrated our thirtieth anniversary, my fiftieth birthday, and my husband's fifty-fifth birthday. Ten years ago, caring for our young family consumed our energy. Now our lives revolve around tweens, teens, and adult children. When I observe people ten years my senior, I conclude that more change will come.

We love the normal flow of "how things are." Change threatens to upset our comfy little worlds because we can't imagine something better. I remember wishing to "freeze my family" at favorite stages. But I would have missed many new, wonderful, and exciting experiences if we could have remained frozen in time.

PATIENCE IS THE *calm acceptance* THAT THINGS CAN HAPPEN IN A DIFFERENT ORDER THAN THE ONE YOU HAVE IN MIND. DAVID G. ALLEN

Ecclesiastes 3:1 says, "To every thing there is a season, and a time to every purpose under the heaven." As homemakers, we need to look for the beauty that comes with changing seasons so we are better prepared to flow with changes that come.

LET CHANGE HAPPEN. Change is continual, and it takes place without our permission. When a routine finally operates smoothly, someone's schedule is sure to change. Even with these changes, homemakers are called to be flexible, keep order, and remain cheerful. These attributes are a stretch for me when well-planned days and weeks are rearranged in a matter of minutes. The best way to embrace change is to flow with daily and seasonal adjustments.

MAINTAIN A HAPPY SPIRIT. Proverbs 17:22, says, "A merry heart doeth good like a medicine." Laughter decreases stress hormones and increases immune cells and infection-fighting antibodies. Laughter prompts the release of endorphins, the body's natural feel-good chemicals. Happy hearts produce a positive outlook, so try a dose of "merry heart" medicine. Sing a song, play a game, or read *Anne of Green Gables*. A conversation with a witty friend usually puts life in perspective.

ADJUST EXPECTATIONS. Exchanging ideals for practicality is one of the hardest things to do. However, the smallest changes can make the biggest difference in how our households flow. For example, my family cannot seem to lift the lid on a clothes hamper. No amount of conversation has revealed why they stack the clothes on the lid or pile them beside the hamper. The only way for clothes to land in the hamper is to keep the lid off and let them dunk the clothes in basketball style. I don't like how it looks, but does that matter? Now I practice my aiming skills too.

SEIZE THE MOMENT. God gives us moments to reach out to bless others. Often these opportunities linger only briefly. It might be an opportunity to speak an encouraging word, build a snowman with a child, or do something kind for a friend or stranger. Embrace the opportunities that a rearranged schedule brings. Arrange your week so you have time to seize the moment while you have the chance. Ask God to help you recognize opportunities; He delights in answering that prayer. It is exciting how God can use ordinary Christian women in extraordinary ways.

TRUST GOD. Some changes are extremely challenging, and we are forced to face things we are not prepared for. The only remedy for these situations is to ask God for wisdom. In James 1:5, He promised His children, "If any of you lack wisdom, let him ask of God, that giveth to all men liberally, and upbraideth not; and it shall be given him." It is truly amazing how God pours wisdom on those who simply ask. *Try it.*

While change is inevitable, we know that God is unchanging. Malachi 3:6 gives us this absolute: "For I am the LORD, I change not." God has promised to give us wisdom, grace, and strength, and He will not change His mind in the middle of our challenges. Courageously embrace change—you will be prepared to flow with the blessings that God has tailored just for you.

ABOUT *Sue*

The Daily Planner was designed by Sue Hooley, wife of Dan for 30 years and mother to six children, two girls and four boys ages 11-27. The planner was developed after several years of motherhood and homemaking. Sue understood that a homemaker's day can rarely be scheduled and structured the same as the one before, nor can every task fit neatly into the time slot allotted by other planners. Since her first publication in 2010, thousands of homemakers have benefited from the Daily Planner.

If you have comments about the Daily Planner, you may share your thoughts by sending an e-mail to: *office@homemakersdepot.com*
or writing to: Sue Hooley P.O. Box 445, Berlin, OH 44610
To read more, visit *www.homemakersdepot.com*

If you like this planner, help us out by leaving a review on Amazon.

NEED A HAND WITH
menu PLANNING?

**Try these Menu Planning Worksheets
at no risk, and . . .**

• Make grocery shopping easier.

• Create balanced meals with more variety.

• Save money by planning in advance.

• Add flexibility to your meal schedule.

• Become more likely to try new recipes.

• Take advantage of sale items.

TO REQUEST YOUR
FREE PRINTABLE PDF,

send an e-mail to: *office@homemakersdepot.com*

or download it from our website at *www.homemakersdepot.com*.

THE FLEXIBLE PLANNER **FOR HOMEMAKERS**

Twenty years ago when I was a young homemaker, I read *Getting More Done in Less Time* by Donna Otto. She recommended using a simple daily planner to keep track of duties, appointments, and commitments. "It will be your friend for life," she promised.

I began my search for a planner that would help me organize my days and duties. But I soon realized that my homemaking days did not fit into neat little time slots. It was frustrating to be rocking the baby at 10:00 when the planner said, "Weed flower bed." So I started designing my own planner pages so that I could have a flexible plan.

Today the *Homemaker's Friend Daily Planner* is a professional version of those homemade pages of years gone by. Through twelve moves, from toddlers to adult children, to mission life in Haiti, this basic, flexible planner kept me on track while allowing me to change from one stage to the next.

> Write with a pencil so tasks can easily be erased and rearranged.

The planner is divided into the following sections.

WEEKLY PLANNING. This user-friendly section helps you make the most out of your week and day. The "Task List" gives you a visual of what needs to be done, and you can divvy out those duties on specific days. Typically, I use a four-week menu plan, but I still write what is for dinner in the menu block.

> Complete the most important tasks first for the day or week to boost productivity.

MONTHLY CALENDAR. This section gives an overall view of events on the horizon. This helps me to be more realistic with weekly planning, since I can see at a glance what will be happening over the next few weeks.

YEARLY CALENDAR. This section has a place for basic notations. Now with the untitled sections, you have a place to journal or write prayer requests, birthdays, and quotes.

> A visual outline of your completed and uncompleted tasks helps you be more organized and stay focused.

TASKS LIST. These pages are untitled to give you the freedom to create monthly, bimonthly, or seasonal lists.

PROJECTS AND EVENTS. This section is for occasions that need more space for writing like when planning a baby shower or a family gathering. Again, these pages are untitled for flexibility.

INFORMATION. This section can be used for phone numbers and addresses that are needed temporarily, such as an address for a card shower or the information for the eye specialist.

> A running shopping list helps you to make the best use of a trip to town.

SHOPPING LISTS. These lists are perforated for your convenience. I use the shopping lists several ways—sometimes as a comprehensive shopping list and other times as a central location for items needed for an upcoming event, project, or menu.

The busier I am, the more I use my planner. It helps me balance homemaking responsibilities with other obligations to create a realistic schedule. Though it is typical for me to veer from a daily plan when urgent matters arise, a written plan refreshes my memory. Mrs. Otto was right—my planner is a lifetime friend.

NEVER FORGET TO ORDER YOUR PLANNER AGAIN!

sign up

FOR AN ANNUAL SUBSCRIPTION

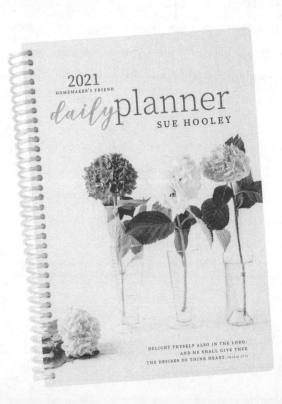

Cross this task off your list once and for all. Sign up for your annual planner subscription, and you'll never need to order another planner. **Anticipate the arrival of your new planner in your mailbox each fall.**

SAVE TIME.

Sign up for an annual subscription to the *Homemaker's Friend Daily Planner*, and we will automatically send you a new planner each fall.

SAVE MONEY.

When you subscribe, you receive a $2.00 discount the first year. Each following year, you get a $1.00 discount off retail price.

Your favorite planner . . . for less.

DO IT ONCE . . .
AND YOU'RE DONE.

As a subscriber, you can count on your new planner arriving each fall, year after year. You can cancel your subscription at any time.

TWO WAYS TO SIGN UP:

1. E-mail *planner@christianlight.org*

2. Call 1-800-776-0478

notes

YEARLY *goals*

DON'T TRY TO RUSH THINGS THAT NEED TIME TO *grow*.

2021 MINI CALENDARS

JANUARY

S	M	T	W	T	F	S
					1	2
3	4	5	6	7	8	9
10	11	12	13	14	15	16
17	18	19	20	21	22	23
24 31	25	26	27	28	29	30

FEBRUARY

S	M	T	W	T	F	S
	1	2	3	4	5	6
7	8	9	10	11	12	13
14	15	16	17	18	19	20
21	22	23	24	25	26	27
28						

MARCH

S	M	T	W	T	F	S
	1	2	3	4	5	6
7	8	9	10	11	12	13
14	15	16	17	18	19	20
21	22	23	24	25	26	27
28	29	30	31			

APRIL

S	M	T	W	T	F	S
				1	2	3
4	5	6	7	8	9	10
11	12	13	14	15	16	17
18	19	20	21	22	23	24
25	26	27	28	29	30	

MAY

S	M	T	W	T	F	S
						1
2	3	4	5	6	7	8
9	10	11	12	13	14	15
16	17	18	19	20	21	22
23 30	24 31	25	26	27	28	29

JUNE

S	M	T	W	T	F	S
		1	2	3	4	5
6	7	8	9	10	11	12
13	14	15	16	17	18	19
20	21	22	23	24	25	26
27	28	29	30			

JULY

S	M	T	W	T	F	S
				1	2	3
4	5	6	7	8	9	10
11	12	13	14	15	16	17
18	19	20	21	22	23	24
25	26	27	28	29	30	31

AUGUST

S	M	T	W	T	F	S
1	2	3	4	5	6	7
8	9	10	11	12	13	14
15	16	17	18	19	20	21
22	23	24	25	26	27	28
29	30	31				

SEPTEMBER

S	M	T	W	T	F	S
			1	2	3	4
5	6	7	8	9	10	11
12	13	14	15	16	17	18
19	20	21	22	23	24	25
26	27	28	29	30		

OCTOBER

S	M	T	W	T	F	S
					1	2
3	4	5	6	7	8	9
10	11	12	13	14	15	16
17	18	19	20	21	22	23
24 31	25	26	27	28	29	30

NOVEMBER

S	M	T	W	T	F	S
	1	2	3	4	5	6
7	8	9	10	11	12	13
14	15	16	17	18	19	20
21	22	23	24	25	26	27
28	29	30				

DECEMBER

S	M	T	W	T	F	S
			1	2	3	4
5	6	7	8	9	10	11
12	13	14	15	16	17	18
19	20	21	22	23	24	25
26	27	28	29	30	31	

2021 DATES TO REMEMBER

JANUARY

_____
_____
_____
_____
_____

FEBRUARY

_____
_____
_____
_____
_____

MARCH

_____
_____
_____
_____
_____

APRIL

_____
_____
_____
_____
_____

MAY

_____
_____
_____
_____
_____

JUNE

_____
_____
_____
_____
_____

JULY

_____
_____
_____
_____
_____

AUGUST

_____
_____
_____
_____
_____

SEPTEMBER

_____
_____
_____
_____
_____

OCTOBER

_____
_____
_____
_____
_____

NOVEMBER

_____
_____
_____
_____
_____

DECEMBER

_____
_____
_____
_____
_____

2022 MINI CALENDARS

JANUARY

S	M	T	W	T	F	S
						1
2	3	4	5	6	7	8
9	10	11	12	13	14	15
16	17	18	19	20	21	22
23 30	24 31	25	26	27	28	29

FEBRUARY

S	M	T	W	T	F	S
		1	2	3	4	5
6	7	8	9	10	11	12
13	14	15	16	17	18	19
20	21	22	23	24	25	26
27	28					

MARCH

S	M	T	W	T	F	S
		1	2	3	4	5
6	7	8	9	10	11	12
13	14	15	16	17	18	19
20	21	22	23	24	25	26
27	28	29	30	31		

APRIL

S	M	T	W	T	F	S
					1	2
3	4	5	6	7	8	9
10	11	12	13	14	15	16
17	18	19	20	21	22	23
24	25	26	27	28	29	30

MAY

S	M	T	W	T	F	S
1	2	3	4	5	6	7
8	9	10	11	12	13	14
15	16	17	18	19	20	21
22	23	24	25	26	27	28
29	30	31				

JUNE

S	M	T	W	T	F	S
			1	2	3	4
5	6	7	8	9	10	11
12	13	14	15	16	17	18
19	20	21	22	23	24	25
26	27	28	29	30		

JULY

S	M	T	W	T	F	S
					1	2
3	4	5	6	7	8	9
10	11	12	13	14	15	16
17	18	19	20	21	22	23
24 31	25	26	27	28	29	30

AUGUST

S	M	T	W	T	F	S
	1	2	3	4	5	6
7	8	9	10	11	12	13
14	15	16	17	18	19	20
21	22	23	24	25	26	27
28	29	30	31			

SEPTEMBER

S	M	T	W	T	F	S
				1	2	3
4	5	6	7	8	9	10
11	12	13	14	15	16	17
18	19	20	21	22	23	24
25	26	27	28	29	30	

OCTOBER

S	M	T	W	T	F	S
						1
2	3	4	5	6	7	8
9	10	11	12	13	14	15
16	17	18	19	20	21	22
23 30	24 31	25	26	27	28	29

NOVEMBER

S	M	T	W	T	F	S
		1	2	3	4	5
6	7	8	9	10	11	12
13	14	15	16	17	18	19
20	21	22	23	24	25	26
27	28	29	30			

DECEMBER

S	M	T	W	T	F	S
				1	2	3
4	5	6	7	8	9	10
11	12	13	14	15	16	17
18	19	20	21	22	23	24
25	26	27	28	29	30	31

2022 DATES TO REMEMBER

JANUARY

_____
_____
_____
_____
_____

FEBRUARY

_____
_____
_____
_____
_____

MARCH

_____
_____
_____
_____
_____

APRIL

_____
_____
_____
_____
_____

MAY

_____
_____
_____
_____
_____

JUNE

_____
_____
_____
_____
_____

JULY

_____
_____
_____
_____
_____

AUGUST

_____
_____
_____
_____
_____

SEPTEMBER

_____
_____
_____
_____
_____

OCTOBER

_____
_____
_____
_____
_____

NOVEMBER

_____
_____
_____
_____
_____

DECEMBER

_____
_____
_____
_____
_____

PERSONALIZE THESE PAGES
for journaling, prayer requests, birthdays, etc.

MONTHLY *goals*

_____

_____

_____

_____

_____

_____

_____

_____

_____

_____

_____

_____

_____

_____

_____

_____

_____

_____

_____

_____

_____

_____

**THE DAY YOU PLANT THE SEED
IS NOT THE DAY YOU EAT THE** *fruit.*

JANUARY

TWO THOUSAND TWENTY-ONE

notes

_____

_____

_____

_____

_____

_____

_____

_____

_____

_____

_____

_____

SUNDAY	MONDAY	TUESDAY
3	4	5
10	11	12
17	18	19
	Martin Luther King Jr. Day	
24	25	26
31		

DECEMBER 20	S	M	T	W	T	F	S
			1	2	3	4	5
	6	7	8	9	10	11	12
	13	14	15	16	17	18	19
	20	21	22	23	24	25	26
	27	28	29	30	31		

FEBRUARY	S	M	T	W	T	F	S
		1	2	3	4	5	6
	7	8	9	10	11	12	13
	14	15	16	17	18	19	20
	21	22	23	24	25	26	27
	28						

WEDNESDAY	THURSDAY	FRIDAY	SATURDAY
		1 New Year's Day	2
6	7	8	9
13	14	15	16
20	21	22	23
27	28	29	30

Cut along dotted line to expose tabs.

FEBRUARY

TWO THOUSAND TWENTY-ONE

notes

SUNDAY	MONDAY	TUESDAY
	1	2 Groundhog Day
7	8	9
14 Valentine's Day	15 Presidents' Day	16
21	22	23
28		

JANUARY

S	M	T	W	T	F	S
					1	2
3	4	5	6	7	8	9
10	11	12	13	14	15	16
17	18	19	20	21	22	23
24 31	25	26	27	28	29	30

MARCH

S	M	T	W	T	F	S
	1	2	3	4	5	6
7	8	9	10	11	12	13
14	15	16	17	18	19	20
21	22	23	24	25	26	27
28	29	30	31			

WEDNESDAY	THURSDAY	FRIDAY	SATURDAY
3	4	5	6
10	11	12	13
17	18	19	20
Ash Wednesday 24	25	26	27

Cut along dotted line to expose tabs.

MARCH

TWO THOUSAND TWENTY-ONE

notes

_____

_____

_____

_____

_____

_____

_____

_____

_____

_____

_____

_____

_____

SUNDAY	MONDAY	TUESDAY
	1	2
7	8	9
14 Daylight Saving Time Begins	15	16
21	22	23
28 Palm Sunday	29	30

FEBRUARY						
S	M	T	W	T	F	S
	1	2	3	4	5	6
7	8	9	10	11	12	13
14	15	16	17	18	19	20
21	22	23	24	25	26	27
28						

APRIL						
S	M	T	W	T	F	S
				1	2	3
4	5	6	7	8	9	10
11	12	13	14	15	16	17
18	19	20	21	22	23	24
25	26	27	28	29	30	

MAR

WEDNESDAY	THURSDAY	FRIDAY	SATURDAY
3	4	5	6
10	11	12	13
17 St. Patrick's Day	18	19	20 Spring Begins
24	25	26	27
31			

Cut along dotted line to expose tabs.

APRIL

notes

_____
_____
_____
_____
_____
_____
_____
_____
_____
_____
_____
_____
_____

SUNDAY	MONDAY	TUESDAY
4	5	6
Easter		
11	12	13
18	19	20
25	26	27

MARCH	S	M	T	W	T	F	S
		1	2	3	4	5	6
	7	8	9	10	11	12	13
	14	15	16	17	18	19	20
	21	22	23	24	25	26	27
	28	29	30	31			

MAY	S	M	T	W	T	F	S
							1
	2	3	4	5	6	7	8
	9	10	11	12	13	14	15
	16	17	18	19	20	21	22
	23 30	24 31	25	26	27	28	29

WEDNESDAY	THURSDAY	FRIDAY	SATURDAY
	1	2 Good Friday	3
7	8	9	10
14	15	16	17
21	22	23	24
28	29	30	

APR

Cut along dotted line to expose tabs.

MAY

notes

SUNDAY	MONDAY	TUESDAY
2	3	4
9	10	11
Mother's Day		
16	17	18
23	24	25
30	31	
	Memorial Day	

APRIL

S	M	T	W	T	F	S
				1	2	3
4	5	6	7	8	9	10
11	12	13	14	15	16	17
18	19	20	21	22	23	24
25	26	27	28	29	30	

JUNE

S	M	T	W	T	F	S
		1	2	3	4	5
6	7	8	9	10	11	12
13	14	15	16	17	18	19
20	21	22	23	24	25	26
27	28	29	30			

WEDNESDAY	THURSDAY	FRIDAY	SATURDAY
			1
5	6	7	8
12	13	14	15
19	20	21	22
26	27	28	29

MAY

Cut along dotted line to expose tabs.

JUNE

notes

SUNDAY	MONDAY	TUESDAY
		1
6	7	8
13	14	15
20	21	22
Father's Day Summer Begins		
27	28	29

MAY

S	M	T	W	T	F	S
						1
2	3	4	5	6	7	8
9	10	11	12	13	14	15
16	17	18	19	20	21	22
23 30	24 31	25	26	27	28	29

JULY

S	M	T	W	T	F	S
				1	2	3
4	5	6	7	8	9	10
11	12	13	14	15	16	17
18	19	20	21	22	23	24
25	26	27	28	29	30	31

WEDNESDAY	THURSDAY	FRIDAY	SATURDAY
2	3	4	5
9	10	11	12
16	17	18	19
23	24	25	26
30			

JUN

Cut along dotted line to expose tabs.

JULY

TWO THOUSAND TWENTY-ONE

SUNDAY	MONDAY	TUESDAY
4 Independence Day	5 Independence Day Observed	6
11	12	13
18	19	20
25	26	27

notes

JUNE

S	M	T	W	T	F	S
		1	2	3	4	5
6	7	8	9	10	11	12
13	14	15	16	17	18	19
20	21	22	23	24	25	26
27	28	29	30			

AUGUST

S	M	T	W	T	F	S
1	2	3	4	5	6	7
8	9	10	11	12	13	14
15	16	17	18	19	20	21
22	23	24	25	26	27	28
29	30	31				

WEDNESDAY	THURSDAY	FRIDAY	SATURDAY
	1	2	3
7	8	9	10
14	15	16	17
21	22	23	24
28	29	30	31

JUL

Cut along dotted line to expose tabs.

AUGUST

TWO THOUSAND TWENTY-ONE

notes

SUNDAY	MONDAY	TUESDAY
1	2	3
8	9	10
15	16	17
22	23	24
29	30	31

JULY	S	M	T	W	T	F	S
					1	2	3
	4	5	6	7	8	9	10
	11	12	13	14	15	16	17
	18	19	20	21	22	23	24
	25	26	27	28	29	30	31

SEPTEMBER	S	M	T	W	T	F	S
				1	2	3	4
	5	6	7	8	9	10	11
	12	13	14	15	16	17	18
	19	20	21	22	23	24	25
	26	27	28	29	30		

WEDNESDAY	THURSDAY	FRIDAY	SATURDAY
4	5	6	7
11	12	13	14
18	19	20	21
25	26	27	28

AUG

Cut along dotted line to expose tabs.

SEPTEMBER

TWO THOUSAND TWENTY-ONE

notes

SUNDAY	MONDAY	TUESDAY
5	6	7
	Labor Day	
12	13	14
19	20	21
26	27	28

AUGUST

S	M	T	W	T	F	S
1	2	3	4	5	6	7
8	9	10	11	12	13	14
15	16	17	18	19	20	21
22	23	24	25	26	27	28
29	30	31				

OCTOBER

S	M	T	W	T	F	S
					1	2
3	4	5	6	7	8	9
10	11	12	13	14	15	16
17	18	19	20	21	22	23
24 31	25	26	27	28	29	30

WEDNESDAY	THURSDAY	FRIDAY	SATURDAY
1	2	3	4
8	9	10	11
15	16	17	18
22	23	24	25
29 Autumn Begins	30		

OCTOBER

notes

_____

_____

_____

_____

_____

_____

_____

_____

_____

_____

_____

_____

_____

_____

SUNDAY	MONDAY	TUESDAY
3	4	5
10	11	12
	Columbus Day	
17	18	19
24	25	26
31		

SEPTEMBER						
S	M	T	W	T	F	S
			1	2	3	4
5	6	7	8	9	10	11
12	13	14	15	16	17	18
19	20	21	22	23	24	25
26	27	28	29	30		

NOVEMBER						
S	M	T	W	T	F	S
	1	2	3	4	5	6
7	8	9	10	11	12	13
14	15	16	17	18	19	20
21	22	23	24	25	26	27
28	29	30				

WEDNESDAY	THURSDAY	FRIDAY	SATURDAY
		1	2
6	7	8	9
13	14	15	16
20	21	22	23
27	28	29	30

OCT

NOVEMBER

notes

_____

_____

_____

_____

_____

_____

_____

_____

_____

_____

_____

_____

_____

SUNDAY	MONDAY	TUESDAY
	1	2
7 Daylight Saving Time Ends	8	9
14	15	16
21	22	23
28	29	30

OCTOBER

S	M	T	W	T	F	S
					1	2
3	4	5	6	7	8	9
10	11	12	13	14	15	16
17	18	19	20	21	22	23
24 31	25	26	27	28	29	30

DECEMBER

S	M	T	W	T	F	S
			1	2	3	4
5	6	7	8	9	10	11
12	13	14	15	16	17	18
19	20	21	22	23	24	25
26	27	28	29	30	31	

WEDNESDAY	THURSDAY	FRIDAY	SATURDAY
3	4	5	6
10	11 Veterans Day	12	13
17	18	19	20
24	25 Thanksgiving Day	26	27

DECEMBER

TWO THOUSAND TWENTY-ONE

notes

SUNDAY	MONDAY	TUESDAY
5	6	7
12	13	14
19	20	21
		Winter Begins
26	27	28

NOVEMBER	S	M	T	W	T	F	S
			1	2	3	4	5	6
	7	8	9	10	11	12	13
	14	15	16	17	18	19	20
	21	22	23	24	25	26	27
	28	29	30				

JANUARY 22	S	M	T	W	T	F	S
							1
	2	3	4	5	6	7	8
	9	10	11	12	13	14	15
	16	17	18	19	20	21	22
	23 30	24 31	25	26	27	28	29

WEDNESDAY	THURSDAY	FRIDAY	SATURDAY
1	2	3	4
8	9	10	11
15	16	17	18
22	23	24 Christmas Eve	25 Christmas Day
29	30	31 New Year's Eve	

DEC

GOALS FOR *january*

_____

_____

_____

_____

_____

_____

_____

_____

_____

_____

SUPPLIES NEEDED/NOTES

_____

_____

_____

_____

_____

_____

_____

_____

GOALS FOR *february*

_____

_____

_____

_____

_____

_____

_____

_____

SUPPLIES NEEDED/NOTES

_____

_____

_____

_____

_____

_____

_____

_____

GOALS FOR *march*

SUPPLIES NEEDED/NOTES

GOALS FOR *april*

SUPPLIES NEEDED/NOTES

GOALS FOR *may*

_____

_____

_____

_____

_____

_____

_____

_____

_____

_____

SUPPLIES NEEDED/NOTES

GOALS FOR *june*

_____

_____

_____

_____

_____

_____

_____

_____

_____

SUPPLIES NEEDED/NOTES

GOALS FOR *july*

_____
_____
_____
_____
_____
_____
_____
_____
_____

SUPPLIES NEEDED/NOTES

_____
_____
_____
_____
_____
_____
_____
_____

GOALS FOR *august*

_____
_____
_____
_____
_____
_____
_____
_____
_____

SUPPLIES NEEDED/NOTES

_____
_____
_____
_____
_____
_____
_____
_____

GOALS FOR *september*

_____
_____
_____
_____
_____
_____
_____
_____
_____

SUPPLIES NEEDED/NOTES

....
....
....
....
....
....
....
....

GOALS FOR *october*

_____
_____
_____
_____
_____
_____
_____
_____
_____

SUPPLIES NEEDED/NOTES

....
....
....
....
....
....
....
....

GOALS FOR *november*

SUPPLIES NEEDED/NOTES

GOALS FOR *december*

SUPPLIES NEEDED/NOTES

MONTHLY RELATIONSHIP GOALS

Have you considered setting monthly goals for your personal relationships?

As homemakers, our relationships with God, our family, and friends are top priority. However, everyday tasks fill our days, and sometimes in the busyness we neglect what we value most.

Perhaps it is easier to set monthly household goals since those tasks are more obvious. We know chaos is pending if we wait to long to organize the game closet or clean the coatroom.

But monthly relationship goals provide relationship awareness even when life is busy. The special things that we do for family, friends, and strangers do make a difference. Sometimes it is in looking back that we understand that the little things we did for others were much bigger than we realized.

Monthly relationship goals help you plan to improve in the areas that need it. They can be custom-made to fit your stage of life. Your personality and circumstances will also shape them. Here are a few ideas to get you started:

AREAS OF FOCUS:	GOAL:
Relationship with God & personal growth	Read a book on prayer
Family	Have a picnic at a park
	Make banana splits
Church & community	Visit Isabella

notes

_____

_____

_____

_____

_____

_____

_____

_____

_____

_____

WEEKLY *goals*

_____

_____

_____

_____

_____

_____

_____

_____

_____

_____

_____

_____

_____

_____

_____

_____

_____

_____

_____

_____

_____

2 PETER 1:5-8

And beside this, giving all diligence,

add to your faith virtue;

and to virtue knowledge; And to knowledge temperance; and to temperance patience;
and to patience godliness; and to godliness brotherly kindness;
and to brotherly kindness charity.
For if these things be in you, and abound, they make you that ye shall neither be
barren nor unfruitful in the knowledge of our Lord Jesus Christ.

tasks list

_____   _____
_____   _____
_____   _____
_____   _____
_____   _____
_____   _____
_____   _____
_____   _____
_____   _____
_____   _____

SEIZE THE MOMENT _____

1 TIMOTHY 1:5

Now the end of the commandment is
charity out of a pure heart,
and of a good conscience, and of faith unfeigned:

DECEMBER						
30	1	2	3	4	5	
6	7	8	9	10	11	12
13	14	15	16	17	18	19
20	21	22	23	24	25	26
27	28	29	30	31		

MONDAY 30

MENU:

TUESDAY 1

MENU:

WEDNESDAY 2

MENU :

THURSDAY 3

MENU :

FRIDAY 4

MENU :

SATURDAY 5

SUNDAY 6

MENU :

MENU :

tasks list

SEIZE THE MOMENT

HEBREWS 11:6

But without faith it is impossible to please him:
for he that cometh to God must believe that he is,
and that he is a rewarder of them that
diligently seek him.

DECEMBER

	1	2	3	4	5
6	7	8	9	10	11	12
13	14	15	16	17	18	19
20	21	22	23	24	25	26
27	28	29	30	31		

MONDAY 7

MENU:

TUESDAY 8

MENU:

WEDNESDAY 9

MENU:

THURSDAY 10

MENU:

FRIDAY 11

MENU:

SATURDAY 12

MENU:

SUNDAY 13

MENU:

tasks list

SEIZE THE MOMENT

JAMES 2:1

My brethren, have not the faith of our
Lord Jesus Christ,
the Lord of glory, with respect of persons.

DECEMBER

		1	2	3	4	5
6	7	8	9	10	11	12
13	14	15	16	17	18	19
20	21	22	23	24	25	26
27	28	29	30	31		

MONDAY 14

MENU:

TUESDAY 15

MENU:

cut here

WEDNESDAY 16

MENU :

THURSDAY 17

MENU :

FRIDAY 18

MENU :

SATURDAY 19

MENU :

SUNDAY 20

MENU :

tasks list

SEIZE THE MOMENT

LUKE 2:14
Glory to God
in the highest, and on earth peace,
good will toward men.

DECEMBER						
		1	2	3	4	5
6	7	8	9	10	11	12
13	14	15	16	17	18	19
20	21	22	23	24	25	26
27	28	29	30	31		

MONDAY 21

WINTER BEGINS

MENU:

TUESDAY 22

MENU:

WEDNESDAY 23

MENU :

THURSDAY 24

CHRISTMAS EVE

MENU :

FRIDAY 25

CHRISTMAS DAY

MENU :

SATURDAY 26

MENU :

SUNDAY 27

MENU :

tasks list

_____ _____
_____ _____
_____ _____
_____ _____
_____ _____
_____ _____
_____ _____
_____ _____
_____ _____

SEIZE THE MOMENT _____

ROMANS 12:10

Be kindly affectioned one to another
with brotherly love;
in honour preferring one another.

JANUARY						
	28	29	30	31	1	2
	3	4	5	6	7	8	9
	10	11	12	13	14	15	16
	17	18	19	20	21	22	23
	24	25	26	27	28	29	30
	31						

MONDAY 28

MENU :

TUESDAY 29

MENU :

cut here

WEDNESDAY 30

MENU:

THURSDAY 31

NEW YEAR'S EVE

MENU:

FRIDAY 1

NEW YEAR'S DAY

MENU:

SATURDAY 2

MENU:

SUNDAY 3

MENU:

tasks list

January 4 » January 10

_____ _____
_____ _____
_____ _____
_____ _____
_____ _____
_____ _____
_____ _____
_____ _____
_____ _____
_____ _____

SEIZE THE MOMENT _____

1 JOHN 3:23

And this is his commandment, That we should
believe on the name of his Son Jesus Christ,
and love one another,
as he gave us commandment.

JANUARY

					1	2
3	4	5	6	7	8	9
10	11	12	13	14	15	16
17	18	19	20	21	22	23
24	25	26	27	28	29	30
31						

MONDAY 4

MENU:

TUESDAY 5

MENU:

WEDNESDAY 6

MENU:

THURSDAY 7

MENU:

FRIDAY 8

MENU:

SATURDAY 9

SUNDAY 10

MENU:

MENU:

tasks list

January 11 » January 17

_____ _____
_____ _____
_____ _____
_____ _____
_____ _____
_____ _____
_____ _____
_____ _____
_____ _____

SEIZE THE MOMENT _____

2 TIMOTHY 2:22

Flee also youthful lusts: but follow righteousness, faith, charity, peace, with them that call on the Lord *out of a pure heart.*

JANUARY

					1	2
3	4	5	6	7	8	9
10	11	12	13	14	15	16
17	18	19	20	21	22	23
24	25	26	27	28	29	30
31						

MONDAY 11

MENU:

TUESDAY 12

MENU:

cut here

WEDNESDAY 13

MENU:

THURSDAY 14

MENU:

FRIDAY 15

MENU:

SATURDAY 16

SUNDAY 17

MENU:

MENU:

tasks list

January 18 » January 24

SEIZE THE MOMENT

JUDGES 6:12, 14
The Lord is with thee,
thou mighty man of valour.
Go in this thy might... have not I sent thee?

JANUARY

					1	2
3	4	5	6	7	8	9
10	11	12	13	14	15	16
17	18	19	20	21	22	23
24	25	26	27	28	29	30
31						

MONDAY 18

MARTIN LUTHER KING JR. DAY

MENU:

TUESDAY 19

MENU:

cut here

WEDNESDAY 20

MENU:

THURSDAY 21

MENU:

FRIDAY 22

MENU:

SATURDAY 23

MENU:

SUNDAY 24

MENU:

tasks list

January 25 » January 31

_____   _____
_____   _____
_____   _____
_____   _____
_____   _____
_____   _____
_____   _____
_____   _____

SEIZE THE MOMENT

HEBREWS 12:14
Follow peace with all men,
and holiness,
without which no man shall see the Lord.

JANUARY						1	2
	3	4	5	6	7	8	9
	10	11	12	13	14	15	16
	17	18	19	20	21	22	23
	24	25	26	27	28	29	30
	31						

MONDAY 25

MENU:

TUESDAY 26

MENU:

WEDNESDAY 27

MENU:

THURSDAY 28

MENU:

FRIDAY 29

MENU:

SATURDAY 30

MENU:

SUNDAY 31

MENU:

tasks list

February 1 » February 7

_____ _____
_____ _____
_____ _____
_____ _____
_____ _____
_____ _____
_____ _____
_____ _____

SEIZE THE MOMENT _____

Jeremiah 9:24
But let him that glorieth glory in this, that he understandeth
and knoweth me, that I am the LORD which exercise
lovingkindness, judgment, and righteousness, in the earth:
for in these things I *delight*, saith the LORD.

FEBRUARY						
	1	2	3	4	5	6
7	8	9	10	11	12	13
14	15	16	17	18	19	20
21	22	23	24	25	26	27
28						

MONDAY 1

MENU:

TUESDAY 2

GROUNDHOG DAY

MENU:

WEDNESDAY 3

MENU:

THURSDAY 4

MENU:

FRIDAY 5

MENU:

SATURDAY 6

MENU:

SUNDAY 7

MENU:

tasks list

February 8 » February 14

_____   _____

_____   _____

_____   _____

_____   _____

_____   _____

_____   _____

_____   _____

_____   _____

_____   _____

SEIZE THE MOMENT _____

PROVERBS 2:10-11

When wisdom entereth into thine heart,
and knowledge is pleasant unto thy soul;
Discretion shall preserve thee,
understanding shall keep thee.

FEBRUARY	1	2	3	4	5	6
7	8	9	10	11	12	13
14	15	16	17	18	19	20
21	22	23	24	25	26	27
28						

MONDAY 8

MENU:

TUESDAY 9

MENU:

WEDNESDAY 10

MENU:

THURSDAY 11

MENU:

FRIDAY 12

MENU:

SATURDAY 13

MENU:

SUNDAY 14

VALENTINE'S DAY

MENU:

tasks list

February 15 » February 21

_____

SEIZE THE MOMENT _____

TITUS 2:2, 3

That the aged men be sober, grave, temperate, sound in faith, in charity, in patience. The aged women likewise, that they be in behaviour as becometh *holiness*, not false accusers, not given to much wine, teachers of good things.

FEBRUARY					
1	2	3	4	5	6
7	8	9	10	11	12	13
14	15	16	17	18	19	20
21	22	23	24	25	26	27
28					

MONDAY 15

PRESIDENTS' DAY

MENU:

TUESDAY 16

MENU:

WEDNESDAY 17

ASH WEDNESDAY

MENU:

THURSDAY 18

MENU:

FRIDAY 19

MENU:

SATURDAY 20

MENU:

SUNDAY 21

MENU:

tasks list

February 22 » February 28

_____   _____
_____   _____
_____   _____
_____   _____
_____   _____
_____   _____
_____   _____
_____   _____
_____   _____

SEIZE THE MOMENT

JAMES 3:13

Who is a wise man and endued with knowledge among you? let him shew out of a good conversation his works with *meekness of wisdom*.

FEBRUARY

		1	2	3	4	5	6
7	8	9	10	11	12	13
14	15	16	17	18	19	20
21	22	23	24	25	26	27
28						

MONDAY 22

MENU:

TUESDAY 23

MENU:

WEDNESDAY 24

MENU:

THURSDAY 25

MENU:

FRIDAY 26

MENU:

SATURDAY 27

MENU:

SUNDAY 28

MENU:

tasks list

March 1 » March 7

_____   _____
_____   _____
_____   _____
_____   _____
_____   _____
_____   _____
_____   _____
_____   _____
_____   _____

SEIZE THE MOMENT _____

PSALM 37:7

Rest in the Lord,
and wait patiently for him: fret not thyself because
of him who prospereth in his way, because of the
man who bringeth wicked devices to pass.

MARCH						
	1	2	3	4	5	6
7	8	9	10	11	12	13
14	15	16	17	18	19	20
21	22	23	24	25	26	27
28	29	30	31			

MONDAY 1

MENU:

TUESDAY 2

MENU:

WEDNESDAY 3

MENU:

THURSDAY 4

MENU:

FRIDAY 5

MENU:

SATURDAY 6

SUNDAY 7

MENU:

MENU:

tasks list

March 8 » March 14

_____   _____
_____   _____
_____   _____
_____   _____
_____   _____
_____   _____
_____   _____
_____   _____
_____   _____

SEIZE THE MOMENT _____

2 THESSALONIANS 3:13
But ye, brethren,
be not weary
in well doing.

MARCH						
	1	2	3	4	5	6
7	8	9	10	11	12	13
14	15	16	17	18	19	20
21	22	23	24	25	26	27
28	29	30	31			

MONDAY 8

MENU:

TUESDAY 9

MENU:

WEDNESDAY 10

MENU:

THURSDAY 11

MENU:

FRIDAY 12

MENU:

SATURDAY 13

MENU:

SUNDAY 14

DAYLIGHT SAVING TIME BEGINS

MENU:

tasks list

_____ _____
_____ _____
_____ _____
_____ _____
_____ _____
_____ _____
_____ _____
_____ _____

SEIZE THE MOMENT _____

JAMES 5:8,9

Be ye also patient;

stablish your hearts: for the coming of the Lord draweth
nigh. Grudge not one against another, brethren, lest ye be
condemned: behold, the judge standeth before the door.

MARCH					
	1	2	3	4	5	6
7	8	9	10	11	12	13
14	15	16	17	18	19	20
21	22	23	24	25	26	27
28	29	30	31			

MONDAY 15

_____
_____
_____
_____
_____   MENU:
_____
_____

TUESDAY 16

_____
_____
_____
_____
_____   MENU:
_____
_____

cut here

WEDNESDAY 17

ST. PATRICK'S DAY

MENU:

THURSDAY 18

MENU:

FRIDAY 19

MENU:

SATURDAY 20

SPRING BEGINS

MENU:

SUNDAY 21

MENU:

tasks list

March 22 » March 28

_____   _____

_____   _____

_____   _____

_____   _____

_____   _____

_____   _____

_____   _____

_____   _____

_____   _____

SEIZE THE MOMENT _____

JAMES 1:5-7

If any of you lack *wisdom*, let him ask of God, that giveth to all men liberally, and upbraideth not; and it shall be given him. But let him ask in faith, nothing wavering... For let not that man think that he shall receive any thing of the Lord.

MARCH						
	1	2	3	4	5	6
7	8	9	10	11	12	13
14	15	16	17	18	19	20
21	22	23	24	25	26	27
28	29	30	31			

MONDAY 22

MENU:

TUESDAY 23

MENU:

cut here

WEDNESDAY 24

MENU:

THURSDAY 25

MENU:

FRIDAY 26

MENU:

SATURDAY 27

MENU:

SUNDAY 28

PALM SUNDAY

MENU:

tasks list

March 29 » April 4

_____   _____
_____   _____
_____   _____
_____   _____
_____   _____
_____   _____
_____   _____
_____   _____
_____   _____

SEIZE THE MOMENT _____

EPHESIANS 4:31

Let all bitterness, and wrath, and anger, and
clamour, and evil speaking,
be put away from you,
with all malice.

APRIL						
	29	30	31	1	2	3
	4	5	6	7	8	9	10
	11	12	13	14	15	16	17
	18	19	20	21	22	23	24
	25	26	27	28	29	30	

MONDAY 29

MENU:

TUESDAY 30

MENU:

WEDNESDAY 31

MENU:

THURSDAY 1

MENU:

FRIDAY 2

GOOD FRIDAY

MENU:

SATURDAY 3

MENU:

SUNDAY 4

EASTER

MENU:

tasks list

April 5 » April 11

_____
_____
_____
_____
_____
_____
_____
_____
_____
_____

SEIZE THE MOMENT _____

COLOSSIANS 3:1

If ye then be risen with Christ,
seek those things which are above,
where Christ sitteth on the right hand of God.

APRIL

				1	2	3
4	5	6	7	8	9	10
11	12	13	14	15	16	17
18	19	20	21	22	23	24
25	26	27	28	29	30	

MONDAY 5

MENU:

TUESDAY 6

MENU:

cut here

WEDNESDAY 7

MENU :

THURSDAY 8

MENU :

FRIDAY 9

MENU :

SATURDAY 10

MENU :

SUNDAY 11

MENU :

tasks list

April 12 » April 18

_____   _____
_____   _____
_____   _____
_____   _____
_____   _____
_____   _____
_____   _____
_____   _____
_____   _____
_____   _____

SEIZE THE MOMENT _____

TITUS 2:12-13

We should live soberly, righteously, and godly,
in this present world;
Looking for that blessed hope,
and the glorious appearing of the great God and our
Saviour Jesus Christ.

APRIL					1	2	3
	4	5	6	7	8	9	10
	11	12	13	14	15	16	17
	18	19	20	21	22	23	24
	25	26	27	28	29	30	

MONDAY 12

_____
_____
_____
_____
_____
_____

MENU:

TUESDAY 13

_____
_____
_____
_____
_____
_____

MENU:

cut here

WEDNESDAY 14

MENU:

THURSDAY 15

MENU:

FRIDAY 16

MENU:

SATURDAY 17

MENU:

SUNDAY 18

MENU:

tasks list

April 19 » April 25

_____   _____
_____   _____
_____   _____
_____   _____
_____   _____
_____   _____
_____   _____
_____   _____

SEIZE THE MOMENT _____

1 TIMOTHY 6:11-12

But thou, O man of God, flee these things; and *follow* after righteousness, godliness, faith, love, patience, meekness. Fight the good fight of faith, lay hold on eternal life.

APRIL

				1	2	3
4	5	6	7	8	9	10
11	12	13	14	15	16	17
18	19	20	21	22	23	24
25	26	27	28	29	30	

MONDAY 19

_____   _____
_____   _____
_____   _____
_____   _____
_____   MENU:
_____
_____

TUESDAY 20

_____   _____
_____   _____
_____   _____
_____   _____
_____   MENU:
_____
_____

WEDNESDAY 21

MENU:

THURSDAY 22

MENU:

FRIDAY 23

MENU:

SATURDAY 24

SUNDAY 25

MENU:

MENU:

tasks list

April 26 » May 2

_____   _____
_____   _____
_____   _____
_____   _____
_____   _____
_____   _____
_____   _____
_____   _____

SEIZE THE MOMENT _____

ROMANS 15:1

We then that are strong
ought to bear the infirmities of the weak,
and not to please ourselves.

APRIL

					1	2	3
4	5	6	7	8	9	10	
11	12	13	14	15	16	17	
18	19	20	21	22	23	24	
25	26	27	28	29	30	1	
2							

MONDAY 26

MENU:

TUESDAY 27

MENU:

cut here

WEDNESDAY 28

MENU:

THURSDAY 29

MENU:

FRIDAY 30

MENU:

SATURDAY 1

MENU:

SUNDAY 2

MENU:

tasks list

May 3 » May 9

SEIZE THE MOMENT

PROVERBS 31:26
She openeth her mouth with wisdom;
and in her tongue is the
law of kindness.

MAY

						1
2	3	4	5	6	7	8
9	10	11	12	13	14	15
16	17	18	19	20	21	22
23	24	25	26	27	28	29
30	31					

MONDAY 3

MENU:

TUESDAY 4

MENU:

WEDNESDAY 5

MENU:

THURSDAY 6

MENU:

FRIDAY 7

MENU:

SATURDAY 8

MENU:

SUNDAY 9

MOTHER'S DAY

MENU:

tasks list

WEEK: 19

May 10 » May 16

_____   _____
_____   _____
_____   _____
_____   _____
_____   _____
_____   _____
_____   _____
_____   _____

SEIZE THE MOMENT _____

EPHESIANS 4:32

And be ye kind one to another,
tenderhearted,
forgiving one another,
even as God for Christ's sake hath forgiven you.

MAY						1
2	3	4	5	6	7	8
9	10	11	12	13	14	15
16	17	18	19	20	21	22
23	24	25	26	27	28	29
30	31					

MONDAY 10

MENU:

TUESDAY 11

MENU:

cut here

WEDNESDAY 12

MENU:

THURSDAY 13

MENU:

FRIDAY 14

MENU:

SATURDAY 15

SUNDAY 16

MENU:

MENU:

tasks list

May 17 » May 23

_____

_____

_____

_____

_____

_____

_____

_____

SEIZE THE MOMENT _____

ACTS 20:35

I have shewed you all things, how that so
labouring ye ought to support the weak,
and to remember the words of the Lord Jesus,
how he said, It is more blessed to *give* than to receive.

MAY

						1
2	3	4	5	6	7	8
9	10	11	12	13	14	15
16	17	18	19	20	21	22
23	24	25	26	27	28	29
30	31					

MONDAY 17

MENU:

TUESDAY 18

MENU:

cut here

WEDNESDAY 19

MENU:

THURSDAY 20

MENU:

FRIDAY 21

MENU:

SATURDAY 22

MENU:

SUNDAY 23

MENU:

tasks list

May 24 » May 30

_____   _____
_____   _____
_____   _____
_____   _____
_____   _____
_____   _____
_____   _____
_____   _____

SEIZE THE MOMENT _____

ROMANS 15:2

Let every one of us
please his neighbour
for his good to edification.

MAY

						1
2	3	4	5	6	7	8
9	10	11	12	13	14	15
16	17	18	19	20	21	22
23	24	25	26	27	28	29
30	31					

MONDAY 24

MENU:

TUESDAY 25

MENU:

WEDNESDAY 26

MENU:

THURSDAY 27

MENU:

FRIDAY 28

MENU:

SATURDAY 29

MENU:

SUNDAY 30

MENU:

tasks list

May 31 » June 6

_____

SEIZE THE MOMENT _____

1 PETER 3:8
Be ye all of one mind,
having compassion one of another,
love as brethren,
be pitiful, be courteous.

JUNE						
	31	1	2	3	4	5
	6	7	8	9	10	11	12
	13	14	15	16	17	18	19
	20	21	22	23	24	25	26
	27	28	29	30			

MONDAY 31

MEMORIAL DAY

MENU:

TUESDAY 1

MENU:

cut here

WEDNESDAY 2

MENU :

THURSDAY 3

MENU :

FRIDAY 4

MENU :

SATURDAY 5

SUNDAY 6

MENU :

MENU :

tasks list

June 7 » June 13

_____   _____
_____   _____
_____   _____
_____   _____
_____   _____
_____   _____
_____   _____
_____   _____
_____   _____

SEIZE THE MOMENT

JAMES 1:27

Pure religion and undefiled before God
and the Father is this, to visit the fatherless
and widows in their affliction, and to keep himself
unspotted from the world.

JUNE		1	2	3	4	5
	6	7	8	9	10	11	12
	13	14	15	16	17	18	19
	20	21	22	23	24	25	26
	27	28	29	30			

MONDAY 7

_____
_____
_____
_____   MENU:
_____
_____

TUESDAY 8

_____
_____
_____
_____   MENU:
_____
_____

cut here

WEDNESDAY 9

MENU:

THURSDAY 10

MENU:

FRIDAY 11

MENU:

SATURDAY 12

MENU:

SUNDAY 13

MENU:

tasks list

June 14 » June 20

_____

SEIZE THE MOMENT _____

EPHESIANS 5:33
Nevertheless let every one of you
in particular so love his wife even as himself;
and the wife see that she
reverence her husband.

JUNE

		1	2	3	4	5
6	7	8	9	10	11	12
13	14	15	16	17	18	19
20	21	22	23	24	25	26
27	28	29	30			

MONDAY 14

MENU:

TUESDAY 15

MENU:

cut here

WEDNESDAY 16

MENU:

THURSDAY 17

MENU:

FRIDAY 18

MENU:

SATURDAY 19

SUNDAY 20

FATHER'S DAY

MENU:

MENU:

tasks list

June 21 » June 27

_____
_____
_____
_____
_____
_____
_____
_____
_____

SEIZE THE MOMENT _____

HOSEA 12:6

Therefore turn thou to thy God:
keep mercy and judgment,
and wait on thy God continually.

JUNE

		1	2	3	4	5
6	7	8	9	10	11	12
13	14	15	16	17	18	19
20	21	22	23	24	25	26
27	28	29	30			

MONDAY 21

SUMMER BEGINS

MENU:

TUESDAY 22

MENU:

WEDNESDAY 23

MENU :

THURSDAY 24

MENU :

FRIDAY 25

MENU :

SATURDAY 26

SUNDAY 27

MENU :

MENU :

tasks list

June 28 » July 4

_____

_____

_____

_____

_____

_____

_____

_____

SEIZE THE MOMENT _____

1 PETER 4:8-9

And above all things have

fervent charity

among yourselves: for charity shall cover the multitude
of sins. Use hospitality one to another without grudging.

JULY						
28	29	30	1	2	3
4	5	6	7	8	9	10
11	12	13	14	15	16	17
18	19	20	21	22	23	24
25	26	27	28	29	30	31

MONDAY 28

MENU:

TUESDAY 29

MENU:

WEDNESDAY 30

MENU:

THURSDAY 1

MENU:

FRIDAY 2

MENU:

SATURDAY 3

MENU:

SUNDAY 4

INDEPENDENCE DAY

MENU:

tasks list

July 5 » July 11

_____   _____
_____   _____
_____   _____
_____   _____
_____   _____
_____   _____
_____   _____
_____   _____
_____   _____

SEIZE THE MOMENT _____

1 THESSALONIANS 3:12
And the Lord make you to
increase and abound
in love one toward another, and toward all men,
even as we do toward you.

JULY

				1	2	3
4	5	6	7	8	9	10
11	12	13	14	15	16	17
18	19	20	21	22	23	24
25	26	27	28	29	30	31

MONDAY 5

INDEPENDENCE DAY OBSERVED

MENU:

TUESDAY 6

MENU:

WEDNESDAY 7

MENU:

THURSDAY 8

MENU:

FRIDAY 9

MENU:

SATURDAY 10

MENU:

SUNDAY 11

MENU:

tasks list

WEEK: 28

July 12 » July 18

_____ _____
_____ _____
_____ _____
_____ _____
_____ _____
_____ _____
_____ _____
_____ _____
_____ _____

SEIZE THE MOMENT _____

JOHN 15:12

This is my commandment,
That ye love one another,
as I have loved you.

JULY						
				1	2	3
4	5	6	7	8	9	10
11	12	13	14	15	16	17
18	19	20	21	22	23	24
25	26	27	28	29	30	31

MONDAY 12

MENU:

TUESDAY 13

MENU:

cut here

WEDNESDAY 14

MENU :

THURSDAY 15

MENU :

FRIDAY 16

MENU :

SATURDAY 17

MENU :

SUNDAY 18

MENU :

tasks list

July 19 » July 25

_____   _____
_____   _____
_____   _____
_____   _____
_____   _____
_____   _____
_____   _____
_____   _____
_____   _____

SEIZE THE MOMENT _____

PSALM 34:14
Depart from evil, and do good;
seek peace,
and pursue it.

JULY

				1	2	3
4	5	6	7	8	9	10
11	12	13	14	15	16	17
18	19	20	21	22	23	24
25	26	27	28	29	30	31

MONDAY 19

MENU:

TUESDAY 20

MENU:

cut here

WEDNESDAY 21

MENU :

THURSDAY 22

MENU :

FRIDAY 23

MENU :

SATURDAY 24

MENU :

SUNDAY 25

MENU :

tasks list

July 26 » August 1

_____
_____
_____
_____
_____
_____
_____
_____
_____

SEIZE THE MOMENT

ROMANS 12:12
Rejoicing in hope;
patient in tribulation;
continuing instant in prayer.

JULY				1	2	3
4	5	6	7	8	9	10
11	12	13	14	15	16	17
18	19	20	21	22	23	24
25	26	27	28	29	30	31
1						

MONDAY 26

MENU:

TUESDAY 27

MENU:

cut here

WEDNESDAY 28

MENU:

THURSDAY 29

MENU:

FRIDAY 30

MENU:

SATURDAY 31

MENU:

SUNDAY 1

MENU:

tasks list

August 2 » August 8

_____   _____
_____   _____
_____   _____
_____   _____
_____   _____
_____   _____
_____   _____
_____   _____
_____   _____

SEIZE THE MOMENT _____

ROMANS 15:5
Now the God of
patience and consolation
grant you to be likeminded one toward another
according to Christ Jesus.

AUGUST	1	2	3	4	5	6	7
	8	9	10	11	12	13	14
	15	16	17	18	19	20	21
	22	23	24	25	26	27	28
	29	30	31				

MONDAY 2

MENU:

TUESDAY 3

MENU:

cut here

WEDNESDAY 4

MENU :

THURSDAY 5

MENU :

FRIDAY 6

MENU :

SATURDAY 7

MENU :

SUNDAY 8

MENU :

tasks list

August 9 » August 15

_____
_____
_____
_____
_____
_____
_____
_____
_____

SEIZE THE MOMENT _____

PSALM 119:165

Great peace
have they which love thy law:
and nothing shall offend them.

AUGUST

1	2	3	4	5	6	7
8	9	10	11	12	13	14
15	16	17	18	19	20	21
22	23	24	25	26	27	28
29	30	31				

MONDAY 9

MENU:

TUESDAY 10

MENU:

WEDNESDAY 11

MENU :

THURSDAY 12

MENU :

FRIDAY 13

MENU :

SATURDAY 14

SUNDAY 15

MENU :

MENU :

tasks list

August 16 » August 22

_____   _____
_____   _____
_____   _____
_____   _____
_____   _____
_____   _____
_____   _____
_____   _____
_____   _____

SEIZE THE MOMENT _____

JAMES 3:17

But the *wisdom* that is from above is first pure,
then peaceable, gentle, and easy to be intreated, full
of mercy and good fruits, without partiality,
and without hypocrisy.

AUGUST

1	2	3	4	5	6	7
8	9	10	11	12	13	14
15	16	17	18	19	20	21
22	23	24	25	26	27	28
29	30	31				

MONDAY 16

MENU:

TUESDAY 17

MENU:

WEDNESDAY 18

MENU :

THURSDAY 19

MENU :

FRIDAY 20

MENU :

SATURDAY 21

SUNDAY 22

MENU :

MENU :

tasks list

August 23 » August 29

_____   _____
_____   _____
_____   _____
_____   _____
_____   _____
_____   _____
_____   _____
_____   _____
_____   _____

SEIZE THE MOMENT _____

JOHN 15:7,8

If ye abide in me, and my words abide in you,
ye shall ask what ye will, and it shall be done unto you.
Herein is my Father glorified, that ye bear much fruit;
so shall ye be my disciples.

AUGUST						
1	2	3	4	5	6	7
8	9	10	11	12	13	14
15	16	17	18	19	20	21
22	23	24	25	26	27	28
29	30	31				

MONDAY 23

MENU:

TUESDAY 24

MENU:

cut here

WEDNESDAY 25

MENU:

THURSDAY 26

MENU:

FRIDAY 27

MENU:

SATURDAY 28

MENU:

SUNDAY 29

MENU:

tasks list

August 30 » September 5

_____   _____
_____   _____
_____   _____
_____   _____
_____   _____
_____   _____
_____   _____
_____   _____
_____   _____

SEIZE THE MOMENT

REMINDER:
Your 2022 Planner is available. *See order form in back.*

DEUTERONOMY 4:9

Only take heed to thyself, and keep thy soul diligently, lest thou forget the things which thine eyes have seen, and lest they depart from thy *heart* all the days of thy life: but teach them thy sons, and thy sons' sons.

SEPTEMBER

30	31	1	2	3	4
5	6	7	8	9	10	11
12	13	14	15	16	17	18
19	20	21	22	23	24	25
26	27	28	29	30		

MONDAY 30

MENU:

TUESDAY 31

MENU:

WEDNESDAY 1

MENU:

THURSDAY 2

MENU:

FRIDAY 3

MENU:

SATURDAY 4

MENU:

SUNDAY 5

MENU:

tasks list

September 6 » September 12

_____ _____
_____ _____
_____ _____
_____ _____
_____ _____
_____ _____
_____ _____
_____ _____
_____ _____
_____ _____

SEIZE THE MOMENT _____

PSALM 77:11,12

I will remember
the works of the LORD:
surely I will remember thy wonders of old. I will
meditate also of all thy work, and talk of thy doings.

SEPTEMBER

				1	2	3	4
5	6	7	8	9	10	11
12	13	14	15	16	17	18
19	20	21	22	23	24	25
26	27	28	29	30		

MONDAY 6

LABOR DAY

MENU:

TUESDAY 7

MENU:

cut here

WEDNESDAY 8

MENU:

THURSDAY 9

MENU:

FRIDAY 10

MENU:

SATURDAY 11

MENU:

SUNDAY 12

MENU:

tasks list

WEEK: 37

September 13 » September 19

_____   _____
_____   _____
_____   _____
_____   _____
_____   _____
_____   _____
_____   _____
_____   _____
_____   _____

SEIZE THE MOMENT

PHILEMON 1:6

That the communication of thy faith may
become effectual by the
acknowledging of every good thing
which is in you in Christ Jesus.

SEPTEMBER

			1	2	3	4
5	6	7	8	9	10	11
12	13	14	15	16	17	18
19	20	21	22	23	24	25
26	27	28	29	30		

MONDAY 13

MENU:

TUESDAY 14

MENU:

cut here

WEDNESDAY 15

MENU:

THURSDAY 16

MENU:

FRIDAY 17

MENU:

SATURDAY 18

MENU:

SUNDAY 19

MENU:

tasks list

September 20 » September 26

_____   _____
_____   _____
_____   _____
_____   _____
_____   _____
_____   _____
_____   _____
_____   _____
_____   _____
_____   _____

SEIZE THE MOMENT _____

COLOSSIANS 4:6

Let your speech be alway with grace,
seasoned with salt,
that ye may know how ye ought to answer every man.

SEPTEMBER

			1	2	3	4
5	6	7	8	9	10	11
12	13	14	15	16	17	18
19	20	21	22	23	24	25
26	27	28	29	30		

MONDAY 20

MENU:

TUESDAY 21

MENU:

WEDNESDAY 22

AUTUMN BEGINS

MENU:

THURSDAY 23

MENU:

FRIDAY 24

MENU:

SATURDAY 25

MENU:

SUNDAY 26

MENU:

tasks list

September 27 » October 3

SEIZE THE MOMENT

COLOSSIANS 4:2
Continue in prayer,
and watch in the same with
thanksgiving.

				1	2	3	4
SEPTEMBER	5	6	7	8	9	10	11
	12	13	14	15	16	17	18
	19	20	21	22	23	24	25
	26	27	28	29	30	1	2
	3						

MONDAY 27

MENU:

TUESDAY 28

MENU:

WEDNESDAY 29

MENU:

THURSDAY 30

MENU:

FRIDAY 1

MENU:

SATURDAY 2

MENU:

SUNDAY 3

MENU:

tasks list

October 4 » October 10

_____   _____
_____   _____
_____   _____
_____   _____
_____   _____
_____   _____
_____   _____
_____   _____
_____   _____

SEIZE THE MOMENT _____

MATTHEW 5:42

Give to him that asketh thee, and from him that would borrow of thee turn not thou away.

OCTOBER						1	2
3	4	5	6	7	8	9	
10	11	12	13	14	15	16	
17	18	19	20	21	22	23	
24	25	26	27	28	29	30	
31							

MONDAY 4

MENU:

TUESDAY 5

MENU:

WEDNESDAY 6

MENU :

THURSDAY 7

MENU :

FRIDAY 8

MENU :

SATURDAY 9

MENU :

SUNDAY 10

MENU :

tasks list

WEEK: 41

October 11 » October 17

_____ _____
_____ _____
_____ _____
_____ _____
_____ _____
_____ _____
_____ _____
_____ _____
_____ _____

SEIZE THE MOMENT _____

MATTHEW 5:44

But I say unto you, *Love* your enemies, bless them that curse you, do good to them that hate you, and pray for them which despitefully use you, and persecute you.

OCTOBER					1	2
3	4	5	6	7	8	9
10	11	12	13	14	15	16
17	18	19	20	21	22	23
24	25	26	27	28	29	30
31						

MONDAY 11

COLUMBUS DAY

MENU:

TUESDAY 12

MENU:

cut here

WEDNESDAY 13

MENU:

THURSDAY 14

MENU:

FRIDAY 15

MENU:

SATURDAY 16

MENU:

SUNDAY 17

MENU:

tasks list

October 18 » October 24

_____   _____
_____   _____
_____   _____
_____   _____
_____   _____
_____   _____
_____   _____
_____   _____

SEIZE THE MOMENT _____

COLOSSIANS 4:5
Walk in wisdom
toward them that are without,
redeeming the time.

OCTOBER						1	2
	3	4	5	6	7	8	9
	10	11	12	13	14	15	16
	17	18	19	20	21	22	23
	24	25	26	27	28	29	30
	31						

MONDAY 18

MENU:

TUESDAY 19

MENU:

WEDNESDAY 20

MENU:

THURSDAY 21

MENU:

FRIDAY 22

MENU:

SATURDAY 23

MENU:

SUNDAY 24

MENU:

tasks list

October 25 » October 31

_____ _____
_____ _____
_____ _____
_____ _____
_____ _____
_____ _____
_____ _____
_____ _____
_____ _____

SEIZE THE MOMENT _____

2 PETER 3:14
Wherefore, beloved, seeing that ye look for such things, be diligent that
ye may be found of him in peace,
without spot, and blameless.

OCTOBER						1	2
3	4	5	6	7	8	9
10	11	12	13	14	15	16
17	18	19	20	21	22	23
24	25	26	27	28	29	30
31						

MONDAY 25

MENU:

TUESDAY 26

MENU:

WEDNESDAY 27

MENU:

THURSDAY 28

MENU:

FRIDAY 29

MENU:

SATURDAY 30

SUNDAY 31

MENU:

MENU:

tasks list

November 1 » November 7

_____   _____
_____   _____
_____   _____
_____   _____
_____   _____
_____   _____
_____   _____
_____   _____
_____   _____

SEIZE THE MOMENT _____

HEBREWS 13:7

Remember them which have the rule over you,
who have spoken unto you the word of God:
whose faith follow,
considering the end of their conversation.

NOVEMBER	1	2	3	4	5	6
	7	8	9	10	11	12	13
	14	15	16	17	18	19	20
	21	22	23	24	25	26	27
	28	29	30				

MONDAY 1

MENU:

TUESDAY 2

MENU:

WEDNESDAY 3

MENU:

THURSDAY 4

MENU:

FRIDAY 5

MENU:

SATURDAY 6

SUNDAY 7

DAYLIGHT SAVING TIME ENDS

MENU:

MENU:

tasks list

November 8 » November 14

_____   _____
_____   _____
_____   _____
_____   _____
_____   _____
_____   _____
_____   _____
_____   _____
_____   _____

SEIZE THE MOMENT _____

1 PETER 3:10,11

For he that will love life, and see good days,
let him refrain his tongue from evil, and his lips
that they speak no guile: Let him eschew evil,
and do good; let him *seek peace*, and ensue it.

NOVEMBER	1	2	3	4	5	6
7	8	9	10	11	12	13
14	15	16	17	18	19	20
21	22	23	24	25	26	27
28	29	30				

MONDAY 8

MENU:

TUESDAY 9

MENU:

cut here

WEDNESDAY 10

MENU:

THURSDAY 11

VETERANS DAY

MENU:

FRIDAY 12

MENU:

SATURDAY 13

MENU:

SUNDAY 14

MENU:

tasks list

November 15 » November 21

_____   _____
_____   _____
_____   _____
_____   _____
_____   _____
_____   _____
_____   _____
_____   _____

SEIZE THE MOMENT _____

1 CORINTHIANS 15:58
Therefore, my beloved brethren, be ye stedfast, unmoveable, always *abounding* in the work of the Lord, forasmuch as ye know that your labour is not in vain in the Lord.

NOVEMBER

	1	2	3	4	5	6
7	8	9	10	11	12	13
14	15	16	17	18	19	20
21	22	23	24	25	26	27
28	29	30				

MONDAY 15

MENU:

TUESDAY 16

MENU:

WEDNESDAY 17

MENU:

THURSDAY 18

MENU:

FRIDAY 19

MENU:

SATURDAY 20

MENU:

SUNDAY 21

MENU:

tasks list

November 22 » November 28

_____   _____

_____   _____

_____   _____

_____   _____

_____   _____

_____   _____

_____   _____

_____   _____

_____   _____

SEIZE THE MOMENT _____

COLOSSIANS 3:14,15

Put on charity,
which is the bond of perfectness. And let the peace
of God rule in your hearts, to the which also ye are
called in one body; and be ye thankful.

NOVEMBER	1	2	3	4	5	6
	7	8	9	10	11	12	13
	14	15	16	17	18	19	20
	21	22	23	24	25	26	27
	28	29	30				

MONDAY 22

MENU:

TUESDAY 23

MENU:

WEDNESDAY 24

MENU :

THURSDAY 25

THANKSGIVING DAY

MENU :

FRIDAY 26

MENU :

SATURDAY 27

MENU :

SUNDAY 28

MENU :

tasks list

November 29 » December 5

_____ _____

_____ _____

_____ _____

_____ _____

_____ _____

_____ _____

_____ _____

_____ _____

SEIZE THE MOMENT _____

2 CORINTHIANS 10:5

Casting down imaginations,
and every high thing that exalteth itself against
the knowledge of God, and bringing into captivity
every thought to the obedience of Christ.

DECEMBER

29	30	1	2	3	4
5	6	7	8	9	10	11
12	13	14	15	16	17	18
19	20	21	22	23	24	25
26	27	28	29	30	31	

MONDAY 29

MENU:

TUESDAY 30

MENU:

WEDNESDAY 1

MENU:

THURSDAY 2

MENU:

FRIDAY 3

MENU:

SATURDAY 4

MENU:

SUNDAY 5

MENU:

tasks list

December 6 » December 12

_____
_____
_____
_____
_____
_____
_____
_____
_____
_____

SEIZE THE MOMENT _____

GALATIANS 5:25,26

If we live in the Spirit, let us also
walk in the Spirit.
Let us not be desirous of vain glory,
provoking one another, envying one another.

DECEMBER

			1	2	3	4
5	6	7	8	9	10	11
12	13	14	15	16	17	18
19	20	21	22	23	24	25
26	27	28	29	30	31	

MONDAY 6

MENU:

TUESDAY 7

MENU:

cut here

WEDNESDAY 8

MENU:

THURSDAY 9

MENU:

FRIDAY 10

MENU:

SATURDAY 11

SUNDAY 12

MENU:

MENU:

tasks list

_____   _____
_____   _____
_____   _____
_____   _____
_____   _____
_____   _____
_____   _____
_____   _____
_____   _____

SEIZE THE MOMENT _____

JAMES 1:12

Blessed is the man that endureth temptation:
for when he is tried, he shall receive the crown of
life, which the Lord hath promised to
them that love him.

DECEMBER						
		1	2	3	4
5	6	7	8	9	10	11
12	13	14	15	16	17	18
19	20	21	22	23	24	25
26	27	28	29	30	31	

MONDAY 13

MENU:

TUESDAY 14

MENU:

cut here

WEDNESDAY 15

MENU:

THURSDAY 16

MENU:

FRIDAY 17

MENU:

SATURDAY 18

SUNDAY 19

MENU:

MENU:

tasks list

_____   _____
_____   _____
_____   _____
_____   _____
_____   _____
_____   _____
_____   _____
_____   _____

SEIZE THE MOMENT _____

ISAIAH 9:6

For unto us a child is born, unto us a son is given: and the government shall be upon his shoulder: and his name shall be called *Wonderful*, Counsellor, The mighty God, The everlasting Father, The Prince of Peace.

DECEMBER

				1	2	3	4
5	6	7	8	9	10	11
12	13	14	15	16	17	18
19	20	21	22	23	24	25
26	27	28	29	30	31	

MONDAY 20

MENU:

TUESDAY 21

WINTER BEGINS

MENU:

WEDNESDAY 22

MENU :

THURSDAY 23

MENU :

FRIDAY 24

CHRISTMAS EVE

MENU :

SATURDAY 25

SUNDAY 26

CHRISTMAS DAY

MENU :

MENU :

cut here

tasks list

December 27, 2021 » Jan. 2, 2022

_____ _____
_____ _____
_____ _____
_____ _____
_____ _____
_____ _____
_____ _____
_____ _____
_____ _____

SEIZE THE MOMENT _____

COLOSSIANS 2:6,7
As ye have therefore received Christ Jesus the Lord, so walk ye in him: Rooted and built up in him, and stablished in the faith, as ye have been taught, abounding therein with *thanksgiving*.

DECEMBER						
			1	2	3	4
5	6	7	8	9	10	11
12	13	14	15	16	17	18
19	20	21	22	23	24	25
26	27	28	29	30	31	1
2						

MONDAY 27

MENU:

TUESDAY 28

MENU:

WEDNESDAY 29

MENU:

THURSDAY 30

MENU:

FRIDAY 31

NEW YEAR'S EVE

MENU:

SATURDAY 1

SUNDAY 2

NEW YEAR'S DAY

MENU:

MENU:

tasks list

_____   _____

_____   _____

_____   _____

_____   _____

_____   _____

_____   _____

_____   _____

_____   _____

_____   _____

SEIZE THE MOMENT _____

GALATIANS 5:22,23

But the fruit of the Spirit is
love, joy, peace,
longsuffering, gentleness, goodness, faith,
meekness, temperance: against such there is no law.

JANUARY						1
2	3	4	5	6	7	8
9	10	11	12	13	14	15
16	17	18	19	20	21	22
23	24	25	26	27	28	29
30	31					

MONDAY 3

MENU:

TUESDAY 4

MENU:

WEDNESDAY 5

MENU:

THURSDAY 6

MENU:

FRIDAY 7

MENU:

SATURDAY 8

SUNDAY 9

MENU:

MENU:

tasks list

_____   _____

_____   _____

_____   _____

_____   _____

_____   _____

_____   _____

_____   _____

_____   _____

SEIZE THE MOMENT _____

1 TIMOTHY 4:12

Let no man despise thy youth; but be thou an
example of the believers,
in word, in conversation, in charity, in spirit,
in faith, in purity.

							1
	2	3	4	5	6	7	8
JANUARY	9	10	11	12	13	14	15
	16	17	18	19	20	21	22
	23	24	25	26	27	28	29
	30	31					

MONDAY 10

_____   _____

_____   _____

_____   _____

_____   M E N U :

_____

TUESDAY 11

_____   _____

_____   _____

_____   _____

_____   M E N U :

_____

WEDNESDAY 12

MENU:

THURSDAY 13

MENU:

FRIDAY 14

MENU:

SATURDAY 15

SUNDAY 16

MENU:

MENU:

notes

tasks list

tasks list

tasks list

tasks list

tasks list

tasks list

tasks list

tasks list

tasks list

tasks list

tasks list

tasks list

tasks list

_____ _____

tasks list

tasks list

tasks list

tasks list

notes

projects + events

projects + events

projects + events

projects + events

projects + events

projects + events

projects + events

projects + events

projects + events

projects + events

projects + events

projects + events

projects + events

projects + events

projects + events

projects + events

projects + events

projects + events

projects + events

projects + events

projects + events

projects + events

notes

information

information

information

information

information

information

notes

SHOPPING *list*

SHOPPING *list*

SHOPPING *list*

SHOPPING
list

SHOPPING
list

SHOPPING
list

SHOPPING list

SHOPPING list

SHOPPING list

SHOPPING
list

SHOPPING
list

SHOPPING
list

SHOPPING
list

SHOPPING
list

SHOPPING
list

SHOPPING list

SHOPPING list

SHOPPING list

SHOPPING
list

SHOPPING
list

SHOPPING
list

SHOPPING
list

SHOPPING
list

SHOPPING
list

SHOPPING list

SHOPPING list

SHOPPING list

SHOPPING
list

SHOPPING
list

SHOPPING
list

SHOPPING *list*

SHOPPING *list*

SHOPPING *list*

SHOPPING list

SHOPPING list

SHOPPING list

SHOPPING list

SHOPPING list

SHOPPING list

SHOPPING list

SHOPPING list

SHOPPING list

SHOPPING list

SHOPPING
list

SHOPPING
list

SHOPPING
list

SHOPPING
list

SHOPPING
list

SHOPPING
list

SHOPPING *list*

SHOPPING *list*

SHOPPING *list*

SHOPPING
list

SHOPPING
list

SHOPPING
list

SHOPPING
list

SHOPPING
list

SHOPPING
list

SHOPPING list

SHOPPING list

SHOPPING list

SHOPPING *list*

SHOPPING *list*

SHOPPING *list*

SHOPPING list

SHOPPING list

SHOPPING list

SHOPPING list

SHOPPING list

SHOPPING list

SHOPPING list

SHOPPING list

SHOPPING list

SHOPPING list

SHOPPING list

SHOPPING list

SHOPPING
list

SHOPPING
list

SHOPPING
list

SHOPPING list

SHOPPING list

SHOPPING list

SHOPPING
list

SHOPPING
list

SHOPPING
list

SHOPPING
list

SHOPPING
list

SHOPPING
list

SHOPPING list

SHOPPING list

SHOPPING list

SHOPPING
list

SHOPPING
list

SHOPPING
list

SHOPPING
list

SHOPPING
list

SHOPPING
list

SHOPPING list

SHOPPING list

SHOPPING list

SHOPPING
list

SHOPPING
list

SHOPPING
list

CLOTHING SIZES

gift IDEAS

grow IN GRACE.

gift IDEAS

WE CAN'T CHANGE PEOPLE,
BUT WE CAN PLANT SEED THAT MAY ONE DAY *bloom* IN THEM.
MARY DAVIS

MASTER SHOPPING LIST

FRUIT	MEAT	BAKING	BREAKFAST

VEGETABLES	FROZEN		BAKERY

PASTA + RICE	DRINKS		MISCELLANEOUS

MASTER SHOPPING LIST

PERSONAL CARE	CLEANING	SEASONINGS	CANS + JARS
	PAPER PRODUCTS	SAUCES + CONDIMENTS	
MEDICATIONS			REFRIGERATED
ANIMALS		CHILDCARE	

MASTER SHOPPING LIST

FRUIT	MEAT	BAKING	BREAKFAST

VEGETABLES	FROZEN		BAKERY

PASTA + RICE	DRINKS		MISCELLANEOUS

MASTER SHOPPING LIST

PERSONAL CARE	CLEANING	SEASONINGS	CANS + JARS
	PAPER PRODUCTS	SAUCES + CONDIMENTS	
MEDICATIONS			REFRIGERATED
ANIMALS		CHILDCARE	

CHECKLIST FOR _____

_____ _____ _____ _____
_____ _____ _____ _____
_____ _____ _____ _____
_____ _____ _____ _____
_____ _____ _____ _____
_____ _____ _____ _____

CHECKLIST FOR _____

_____ _____ _____ _____
_____ _____ _____ _____
_____ _____ _____ _____
_____ _____ _____ _____
_____ _____ _____ _____
_____ _____ _____ _____

CHECKLIST FOR _____

_____ _____ _____ _____
_____ _____ _____ _____
_____ _____ _____ _____
_____ _____ _____ _____
_____ _____ _____ _____

CHECKLIST FOR _____

_____ _____ _____ _____
_____ _____ _____ _____
_____ _____ _____ _____
_____ _____ _____ _____
_____ _____ _____ _____
_____ _____ _____ _____

CHECKLIST FOR _____

_____ _____ _____ _____
_____ _____ _____ _____
_____ _____ _____ _____
_____ _____ _____ _____
_____ _____ _____ _____
_____ _____ _____ _____

CHECKLIST FOR _____

_____ _____ _____ _____
_____ _____ _____ _____
_____ _____ _____ _____
_____ _____ _____ _____
_____ _____ _____ _____
_____ _____ _____ _____

ORDER FORM

To order, send this completed order form to:

CHRISTIAN LIGHT PUBLICATIONS

P.O. Box 1212 . Harrisonburg, VA 22803-1212

Phone: 1-800-776-0478 · 8:30-5:00 EST

Fax: 540-433-8896 · E-mail: planner@christianlight.org · Web: www.christianlight.org

Name _____   Date _____

Mailing Address _____   Phone _____

City _____ State _____ Zip _____

2021 Daily Planner   Qty. _____ x $15.99 ea. = _____

2022 Daily Planner   Qty. _____ x $15.99 ea. = _____

(Prices subject to change without notice)

☐ **Check here to sign up for an automatic annual subscription to this planner. Subtract $2.00 from the order subtotal. We will charge your credit card annually when shipping your new planner. You may cancel at any time.**

Order Summary

Order Subtotal _____ A

Subtract for Subscription _____ B

VA (5.3%) or PA (6.0%) Tax
(based on A) • (VA & PA residents only) + _____ C

Shipping
• Orders up to $44.50 add $4.00
• Orders $44.51 and over add 9% of A + _____ D

TOTAL of A -D _____

All Payments in US Dollars

☐ Check/Money Order   ☐ Visa

☐ MasterCard   ☐ Discover   ☐ American Express

Name on Card _____

_____ - _____ - _____ - _____

Charge Card Number

_____   _____

Exp. Date   Signature

For orders shipping outside the United States, please give us a call.

THANK YOU FOR YOUR ORDER!

THANK YOU
FOR CHOOSING THE

2021
HOMEMAKER'S FRIEND
*daily*planner
SUE HOOLEY